Emma & Egor

Signing Exact English

Emma

Eli

Egor

This Book is dedicated to Tyler and Alexandra:

Thank you for being my ongoing inspiration in creating
a Signing Exact English educational program that will positively
impact the education and development of ALL children.

Winter   Spring   Summer   Fall

twice

Yesterday   Today   Tomorrow

to

day

Sunny   Windy   Cloudy   Rainy   Snowy

1 sun

1 wind

1 snow

2 -y

2 -y

1 cloud

2 -y

1 rain

2 -y

2 -y

3

There are four SEASONS

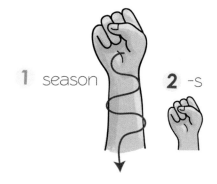

1 season   **2** -s

in a YEAR

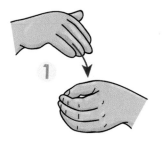

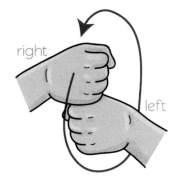

right

left

WINTER

SPRING

twice

SUMMER

FALL

5

The WINTER months are

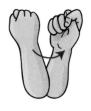  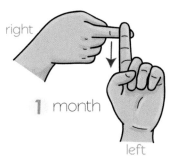  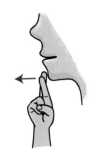

DECEMBER

FEBRUARY

JANUARY

WINTER is cold. Emma loves winter

What do you think the weather

is like in the WINTER ?

Snowy

1 snow

2 -y

Sunny

1 sun

2 -y

Windy

1 wind

2 -y

Cloudy

1 cloud

2 -y

What do you think Emma

should do on this snowy day ?

Ski and

Snowboard

snow

board

Play outside

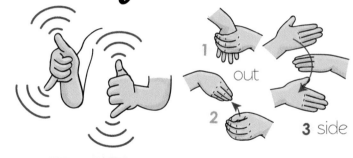

out

1

2

3 side

Ice Skate

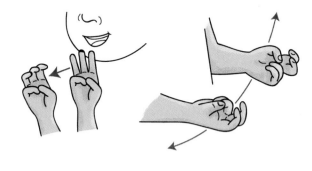

Sled

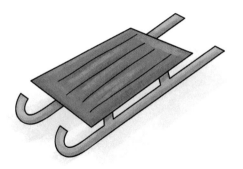

It is too cold to go outside.

What should Emma do ?

Drink hot

chocolate

Sit by the

fire

Make puzzles

touch and twist

puzzle

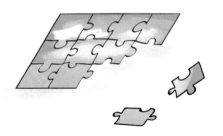

Color and draw

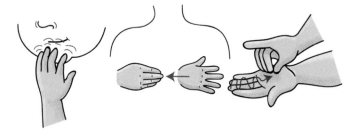

The SPRING months are

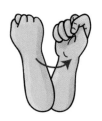 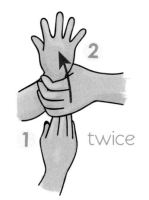

twice

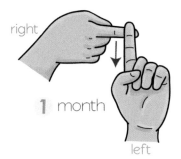

1 month
left

2 -s

 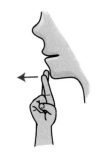

MARCH

right   left

APRIL

right   left

MAY

1 "M"

right   left

2 "Y"

14

Egor   is   happy   it   is   SPRING

What do you think the weather

is like in the SPRING ?

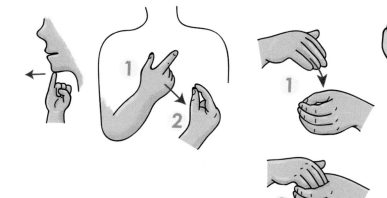

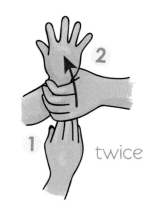

twice

Sunny

1 sun

2 -y

Rainy

1 rain

2 -y

Windy

1 wind

2 -y

Snowy

1 snow

2 -y

What do you think Egor

should do on this sunny day ?

1 sun

2 -y

Plant a Garden

Ride Bikes

Go to the Zoo

Fly a Kite

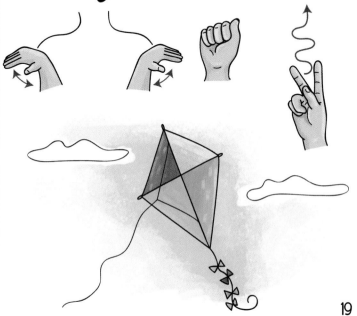

19

Today is a rainy SPRING day,

What do you think Egor should do?

Read a book

Play a game

Play in the

rain

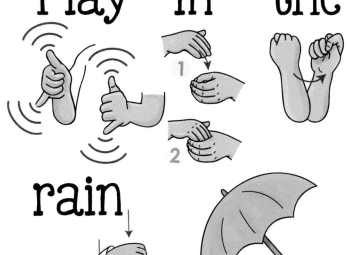

Bake cookies

cookie

21

The SUMMER months are

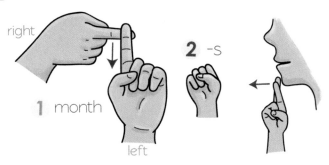

1 month 2 -s

JUNE

JULY

AUGUST

1 "J" right   left   2 "E"

1 "J" right   left   2 "Y"

1 "A" right   left   2 "G"

Emma, Egor and Eli love to

play together in the SUMMER

Sometimes

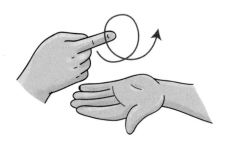

SUMMER

weather

can

be

Hot

Cloudy

1 cloud

2 -y

Sunny

1 sun

2 -y

Rainy

2 -y

1 rain

25

What should Emma and Egor

  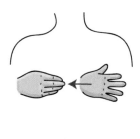 

do on this SUMMER day ?

Ride bikes

Swim

Go to the

beach

Play soccer

The FALL months are

 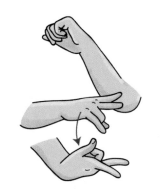 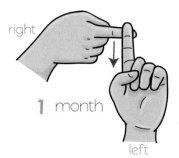  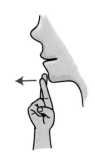

right

1 month

left

2 -s

SEPTEMBER NOVEMBER
OCTOBER

right   left

right   left

right   left

Emma, Egor and Eli are going

back to school.

What kind of weather do

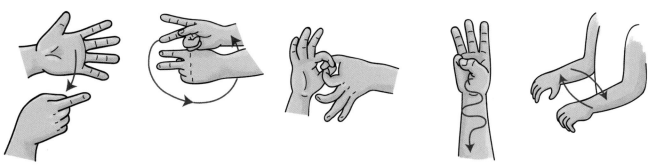

we have in the FALL ?

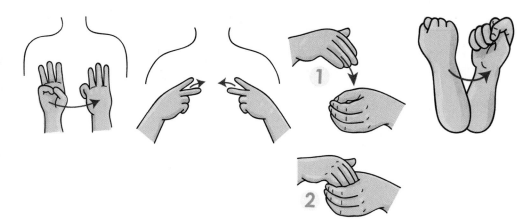

Sunny

1 sun

2 -y

Cloudy

1 cloud

2 -y

Windy

1 wind

2 -y

Rainy

1 rain

2 -y

What do you like to

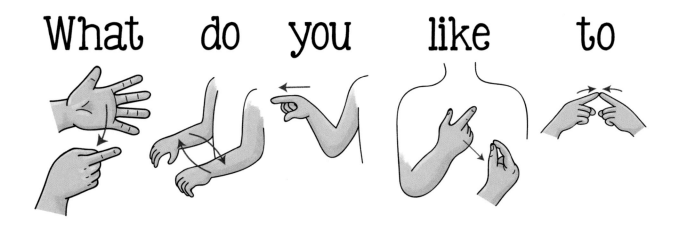

do in the FALL ?

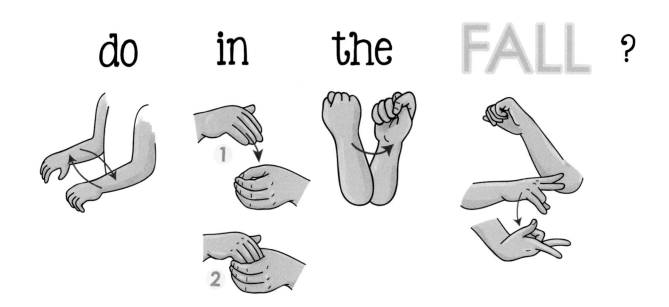

Pick berries

2 -s **1** berry

and apples

1 apple **2** -s

Carve pumpkins

2 -s **1** pumpkin

Go to the

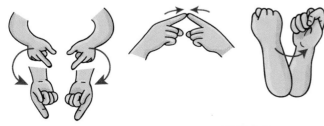

farm

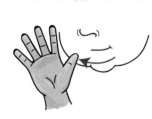

Go hiking

1 hike **2** -ing

Egor wants to know what

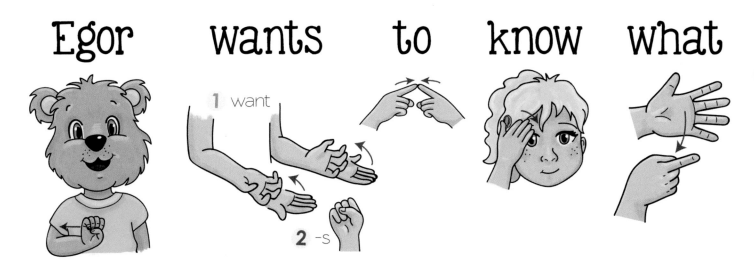

season you like best ?

  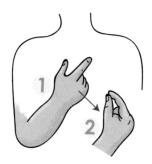 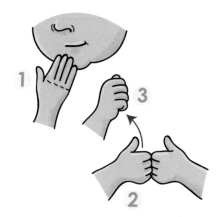

WINTER

SPRING

twice

SUMMER

FALL

35

What is the weather

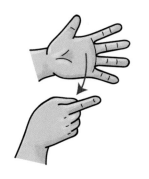  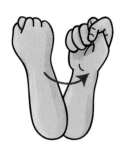 

like today ?

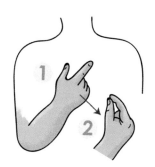 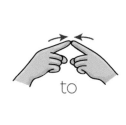 

Sunny

1 sun
2 -y

Cloudy

1 cloud
2 -y

Windy

1 wind
2 -y

Snowy

1 snow
2 -y

Rainy

1 rain
2 -y

37

The   End

About the Author

Stacy Eldred searched for years to find resource books and teaching tutorials for her Deaf/Hard of Hearing daughter. After teaching sign language to toddlers and preschoolers for over 10 years, she decided it was time to create a fun, easy, instructive and interactive way for teachers and parents to teach SEE (Signing Exact English) to hearing and non-hearing children. Thus Emma and Egor were born.

Stacy resides in Northern Virginia and had been developing her sign language skills for 21 years. Her passion is educating and nurturing the minds of children all over the world. It is her goal to reach as many people as possible through Emma and Egor.

About the Illustrator

Lucía Benito was born in Buenos Aires, Argentina, and has been drawing ever since she can remember. She has illustrated many children's books, as well as material for raising public awareness on environmental and social issues.

She considers herself blessed to be able to work at something she loves and in which she excels. In her own words:

"I truly believe that the greatest joy of being a graphic artist is to witness the happiness of the writer when they see their written words turn into images that had only existed in their imagination."

You can see more of her work at: www.tuolvidastodo.com

Made in the
USA
Middletown, DE